AF437880

IN HELL CAME A PRAY, PRAISE, GLORY OF GOD IN HELL

Willie J. Brown

ISBN 979-8-88685-379-7 (paperback)
ISBN 979-8-88685-380-3 (digital)

Copyright © 2023 by Willie J. Brown

All rights reserved. No part of this publication may be reproduced, distributed, or transmitted in any form or by any means, including photocopying, recording, or other electronic or mechanical methods without the prior written permission of the publisher. For permission requests, solicit the publisher via the address below.

Christian Faith Publishing
832 Park Avenue
Meadville, PA 16335
www.christianfaithpublishing.com

Printed in the United States of America

We in this life go through so much trials and tribulations. There are others who go through hell or being in a hell situation, they see no way out of the darkness.

Why should we praise God after we pray and when we are in the midst of trouble? When things are going the wrong way and it looks like it has gotten worse? When you are standing on his word, waiting on the manifestation? Praise His Holy name, giving thanks that it is already done in the name of Jesus Christ. Jesus was born in a time where there weren't police officers or any system to protect family from harm. In Jesus's time, there was King Herod who put out a decree that all children two years old and under be put to death all in Bethlehem and the whole cost. An angel appeared to Joseph in a dream, telling him to flee to Egypt with Mary and the **infant Jesus** since King Herod would seek the child to kill him.

> And when they were departed, behold, the angel of the Lord appeareth to Joseph in a dream, saying, Arise, and take the young child and his mother, and flee into Egypt, and be thou there until I bring thee word: for Herod will seek the young child to destroy him. When he arose, he took the young child and his mother by night, and departed into Egypt: And was there until the death of Herod: that it might be fulfilled which was spoken of the Lord by the prophet, saying, Out of Egypt have I called my son. Then Herod, when he saw that he was mocked of the wise men, was exceeding wroth, and sent forth, and slew all the children that were in Bethlehem, and in all the coasts thereof, from two years old and under, according to the time which he had diligently enquired of the wise men. Then was fulfilled that which was spoken by Jeremiah the

prophet, saying, In Rama was there a voice heard, lamentation, and weeping, and great mourning, Rachel weeping for her children, and would not be comforted, because they are not. But when Herod was dead, behold, an angel of the Lord appeareth in a dream to Joseph in Egypt, Saying, Arise, and take the young child and his mother, and go into the land of Israel: for they are dead which sought the young child's life. (Matthew 2:13–20 KJV)

When Jesus was thirty, He started his ministry after the baptism of John the Baptist.

Then cometh Jesus from Galilee to Jordan unto John, to be baptized of him. But John forbad him, saying, I have need to be baptized of thee, and comest thou to me? And Jesus answering said unto him, Suffer it to be so now: for thus it becometh us to fulfil all righteousness. Then he suffered him. And Jesus, when he was baptized, went up straightway out of the water: and, lo, the heavens were opened unto him, and he saw the Spirit of God descending like a dove, and lighting upon him: And lo a voice from heaven, saying, This is my beloved Son, in whom I am well pleased. (Matthew 3:13–17 KJV)

And Jesus being full of the Holy Ghost returned from Jordan, and was led by the Spirit into the wilderness, Being forty days tempted of the devil. And in those days he did eat nothing: and when they were ended, he afterward hungered. And the devil said unto him, If thou be the Son of God, command this stone that it be made bread. And Jesus answered him, saying, It is written, That

man shall not live by bread alone, but by every
word of God. And the devil, taking him up into
an high mountain, shewed unto him all the kingdoms of the world in a moment of time. And
the devil said unto him, All this power will I give
thee, and the glory of them: for that is delivered
unto me; and to whomsoever I will I give it. If
thou therefore wilt worship me, all shall be thine.
And Jesus answered and said unto him, Get thee
behind me, Satan: for it is written, Thou shalt
worship the Lord thy God, and him only shalt
thou serve. And he brought him to Jerusalem,
and set him on a pinnacle of the temple, and said
unto him, If thou be the Son of God, cast thyself
down from hence: For it is written, He shall give
his angels charge over thee, to keep thee: And in
their hands they shall bear thee up, lest at any
time thou dash thy foot against a stone. And
Jesus answering said unto him, It is said, Thou
shalt not tempt the Lord thy God. (Luke 4:1–12
KJV)

Look at these verses. The devil said, "If thou be the son of God."
But God said, "This is my beloved Son."

We are the beloved sons of God, not just the Son of God. God
is so in love with us.

And then, the devil took Jesus to a high mountain and showed
Him all the kingdoms in a moment. "All this power will I give thee,
and the glory of them: for that is delivered unto me; that's the power
he got after the fall Adam had"; that was the main thing Jesus was
after. This was a great temptation for Jesus. He came to get back what
the devil stole that belonged to us. God will restore everything the
devil took from you and will double what was taken from you.

Instead of your shame you will receive a double
portion, and instead of disgrace you will rejoice

> in your inheritance. And so you will inherit a
> double portion in your land, and everlasting joy
> will be yours. (Isaiah 61:7 NIVUK)

Jesus did great sign and wonders and miracle among the people, but then came the time for Jesus Christ to die for the whole world, for our sins.

> And he said, Go into the city to such a man, and say unto him, The Master saith, My time is at hand; I will keep the passover at thy house with my disciples. And the disciples did as Jesus had appointed them; and they made ready the passover. Now when the even was come, he sat down with the twelve. And as they did eat, he said, Verily I say unto you, that one of you shall betray me. And they were exceeding sorrowful, and began every one of them to say unto him, Lord, is it I? And he answered and said, He that dippeth his hand with me in the dish, the same shall betray me. The Son of man goeth as it is written of him: but woe unto that man by whom the Son of man is betrayed! it had been good for that man if he had not been born. Then Judas, which betrayed him, answered and said, Master, is it I? He said unto him, Thou hast said. (Matthew 26:18–25 KJV)

At that time, Jesus gave Judas time to repent, but he did not. God's grace is all there when you do wrong. No matter what it is, God's love and mercy are always here to restore you.

The gospels of Matthew and Mark identify this place of prayer as **Gethsemane**. During His agony, **Jesus** prayed. "His sweat was as **it were** great drops of blood falling down upon the ground" (Luke 22:44). At the conclusion of the narrative, **Jesus** accepts that the hour **has** come for Him to be betrayed.

Look at when Jesus and the disciples were at the Garden of Gethsemane.

> And he was withdrawn from them about a stone's cast, and kneeled down, and prayed, Saying, Father, if thou be willing, remove this cup from me: nevertheless not my will, but thine, be done. And there appeared an angel unto him from heaven, strengthening him."
>
> Father, if thou be willing, remove this cup from me: nevertheless not my will, but thine, be done. And there appeared an angel unto him from heaven, strengthening him. (Luke 23:41–44)

> And being in an agony he prayed more earnestly: and his sweat was as it were great drops of blood falling down to the ground. And when he rose up from prayer, and was come to his disciples, he found them sleeping for sorrow, And said unto them, Why sleep ye? rise and pray, lest ye enter into temptation. And while he yet spake, behold a multitude, and he that was called Judas, one of the twelve, went before them, and drew near unto Jesus to kiss him. But Jesus said unto him, Judas, betrayest thou the Son of man with a kiss? (Luke 22:44–48 KJV)

Judas throw away love with kiss, but Jesus love Him so When

Jesus went through a tremendous ordeal before the cross. The Roman guards beat him with a cat-o'-nine-tails, ripping open His flesh. The Bible mentioned He didn't even look human. He looked like a piece of raw meat that had been beaten by a meat mallet. On the cross, before He said "It is finished," it was dark for three hours. During that time, every sin that man has done, every sickness and diseases, and every punishment that we were supposed to pay for came upon Jesus, the sins of the whole world. Even in death, Jesus turned into a serpent up on the cross, having all the sins of the whole world. That was why Thomas said, "I will not believe, except I see the print of the nails and put my finger into the print of the nails and thrust my hand into his side. I will not believe."

> But Thomas, one of the twelve, called Didymus, was not with them when Jesus came. The other disciples therefore said unto him, We have seen the Lord. But he said unto them, Except I shall see in his hands the print of the nails, and put my finger into the print of the nails, and thrust my hand into his side, I will not believe. And after eight days again his disciples were within, and Thomas with them: then came Jesus, the doors being shut, and stood in the midst, and said, Peace be unto you. Then saith he to Thomas, Reach hither thy finger, and behold my hands; and reach hither thy hand, and thrust it into my side: and be not faithless, but believing. And Thomas answered and said unto him, My Lord and my God. Jesus saith unto him, Thomas, because thou hast seen me, thou hast believed: blessed are they that have not seen, and yet have believed. (John 20:24–29 KJV)

He saw what Jesus looked like with all the sins of the world, every sickness and diseases, every poverty and lack, and every curse that was put on mankind. This was how the sins of the whole world looked like on Jesus. He looked like a serpent. The Bible foretells of Jesus on the cross in the book of Numbers 21:5–8. Let's look at it:

> And the people spake against God, and against Moses, Wherefore have ye brought us up out of Egypt to die in the wilderness? for there is no

bread, neither is there any water; and our soul loatheth this light bread. And the Lord sent fiery serpents among the people, and they bit the people; and much people of Israel died. Therefore the people came to Moses, and said, We have sinned, for we have spoken against the Lord, and against thee; pray unto the Lord, that he take away the serpents from us. And Moses prayed for the people. And the Lord said unto Moses, Make thee a fiery serpent, and set it upon a pole: and it shall come to pass, that every one that is bitten, when he looketh upon it, shall live. (John 20:24–29 KJV)

That's why Thomas did not believe.

The other disciples said, "We saw the Lord." Thomas has seen in the Spirit what Jesus really looked like. He looked like a serpent on the cross. It was so imbedded in his mind that he could not get it out. This was after Jesus was told by one of the thieves to remember him when He comes into His kingdom. There was darkness over the whole earth for three hours. During this event, there was a change in the atmosphere. Darkness was over the whole earth, and then lightning struck across the sky. That's when Thomas saw all the sins of the world—even death—all of it, on Jesus. He paid the price for it all, every bit of it.

> And about the ninth hour Jesus cried with a loud voice, saying, Eli, Eli, lama sabachthani? that is to say, My God, my God, why hast thou forsaken me? (Matthew 27:46 KJV)

Then He said, "It is finished."

> When Jesus therefore had received the vinegar, he said, It is finished: and he bowed his head, and gave up the ghost. (John 19:30 KJV)

But this say in between (my God Why hast thou forsaken me) and (it is finish), Jesus was saying

MY GOD, my God, why have You forsaken me? Why are You so far from helping me, and from the words of my groaning? [Matt. 27:46.] O my God, I cry in the daytime, but You answer not; and by night I am not silent or find no rest. But You are holy, O You Who dwell in [the holy place where] the praises of Israel [are offered]. Our fathers trusted in You; they trusted (leaned on, relied on You, and were confident) and You delivered them. They cried to You and were delivered; they trusted in, leaned on, and confidently relied on You, and were not ashamed or confounded or disappointed. But I am a worm, and no man; I am the scorn of men, and despised by the people. [Matt. 27:39-44.] All who see me laugh at me and mock me; they shoot out the lip, they shake the head, saying, [Matt. 27:43.] He trusted and rolled himself on the Lord, that He would deliver him. Let Him deliver him, seeing that He delights in him! [Matt. 27:39, 43; Mark 15:29, 30; Luke 23:35.] Yet You are He Who took me out of the womb; You made me hope and trust when I was on my mother's breasts. I was cast upon You from my very birth; from my mother's womb You have been my God. Be not far from me, for trouble is near and there is none to help. Many [foes like] bulls have surrounded me; strong bulls of Bashan have hedged me in. [Ezek. 39:18.] Against me they opened their mouths wide, like a ravening and roaring lion. I am poured out like water, and all my bones are out of joint. My heart is like wax; it is softened [with anguish] and melted down within me. My strength is dried up like a fragment of clay pottery; [with thirst] my tongue cleaves to my jaws; and You have brought me into the dust of death. [John 19:28.] For [like a pack of] dogs they have encompassed me; a company of evildoers has encircled me, they pierced my hands and my feet. [Isa. 53:7; John 19:37.] I can count all my bones; [the evildoers] gaze at me. [Luke 23:27, 35.] They part my clothing among them and cast lots for my raiment (a long, shirtlike garment, a seamless undertunic). [John 19:23, 24.]) But be not far from me, O Lord; O my Help, hasten to aid me! Deliver my life from the sword, my dear life [my only one] from the power of the dog [the agent of execution]. Save me from the lion's mouth; for You have answered me [kindly] from the horns of the wild oxen. I will declare Your name to my brethren; in the midst of the congregation will I praise You. [John 20:17; Rom. 8:29; Heb. 2:12.] You who fear (revere and worship) the Lord, praise Him! All you offspring of Jacob, glorify Him. Fear (revere and worship) Him, all you offspring of Israel. For He has not despised or abhorred the affliction of the afflicted; neither has He hidden His face from him, but when he cried to Him, He heard. My praise shall be of You in the great congregation. I will pay to Him my vows [made in the time of trouble] before them who fear (revere and worship) Him. The poor and afflicted shall eat and be satisfied; they shall praise the Lord—they who [diligently] seek for, inquire of and for Him, and require Him [as their greatest need]. May your hearts be quickened now and forever! All the ends of the earth shall remember and turn to the Lord, and all the families of the nations shall bow down and worship before You, For the kingship and the kingdom are the Lord's, and He is the ruler over the nations. All the mighty ones upon earth shall eat [in thanksgiving] and worship; all they that go down to the dust shall bow before Him, even he who cannot keep himself alive. Posterity shall serve Him; they shall tell of the Lord to the next generation. They shall come and shall declare His righteousness to a people yet to be born—that He has done it [that it is finished]! [John 19:30]. (Psalm 22:1–31 AMPC)

Then on the third day, the Holy Spirit came down from heaven, piercing through the earth and in hell, and landed upon Jesus the same way as when He was baptized by John in the beginning of His ministry. The Holy Spirit was a seal, a promise the God would not leave Jesus in hell. Jesus was the only man born again in hell. The power of the Holy Ghost was upon Jesus, and He made a show of them openly.

And having spoiled principalities and powers, he made a shew of them openly, triumphing over them in it. (Colossians 2:15 KJV)

The saints of old were trapped down there in hell.

There was a certain rich man, which was clothed in purple and fine linen, and fared sumptuously every day: And there was a certain beggar named Lazarus, which was laid at his gate, full of sores, And desiring to be fed with the crumbs which fell from the rich man's table: moreover the dogs came and licked his sores. And it came to pass, that the beggar died, and was carried by the angels into Abraham's bosom: the rich man also died, and was buried; And in hell he lift up his eyes, being in torments, and seeth Abraham afar off, and Lazarus in his bosom. And he cried and said, Father Abraham, have mercy on me, and send Lazarus, that he may dip the tip of his finger in water, and cool my tongue; for I am tormented in this flame. But Abraham said, Son, remember that thou in thy lifetime receivedst thy good things, and likewise Lazarus evil things: but now he is comforted, and thou art tormented. And beside all this, between us and you there is a great gulf fixed: so that they which would pass from hence to you cannot; neither can they pass to us, that would come from thence. Then he said, I pray thee therefore, father, that thou wouldest send him to my father's house: For I have five brethren; that he may testify unto them, lest they also come into this place of torment. Abraham saith unto him, They have Moses and the prophets; let them hear them. And he said, Nay, father Abraham: but if one went unto them from the dead, they will repent. And he said unto him, If they hear not Moses and the prophets, neither will they be persuaded, though one rose from the dead. (Luke 16:19-31 KJV)

Everyone who died in God's name but were trapped in hell was carried to Paradise, which God had protected with cherubim and a flaming sword.

And the Lord God said, Behold, the man is become as one of us, to know good and evil: and now, lest he put forth his hand, and take also of the tree of life, and eat, and live for ever: Therefore the Lord God sent him forth from the garden of Eden, to till the ground from whence he was taken. So he drove out the man;

and he placed at the east of the garden of Eden Cherubims, and a flaming sword which turned every way, to keep the way of the tree of life. (Genesis 3:22–24 KJV)

Ye men of Israel, hear these words; Jesus of Nazareth, a man approved of God among you by miracles and wonders and signs, which God did by him in the midst of you, as ye yourselves also know: Him, being delivered by the determinate counsel and foreknowledge of God, ye have taken, and by wicked hands have crucified and slain: Whom God hath raised up, having loosed the pains of death: because it was not possible that he should be holden of it. For David speaketh concerning him, I foresaw the Lord always before my face, for he is on my right hand, that I should not be moved: Therefore did my heart rejoice, and my tongue was glad; moreover also my flesh shall rest in hope: Because thou wilt not leave my soul in hell, neither wilt thou suffer thine Holy One to see corruption. Thou hast made known to me the ways of life; thou shalt make me full of joy with thy countenance. (Acts 2:22–28 KJV)

David and all who died whom God used for His glory were trapped down there in hell, but Jesus came to set them free.

And a superscription also was written over him in letters of Greek, and Latin, and Hebrew, THIS IS THE KING OF THE JEWS. And one of the malefactors which were hanged railed on him, saying, If thou be Christ, save thyself and us. But the other answering rebuked him, saying, Dost not thou fear God, seeing thou art in the same condemnation? And we indeed justly; for we receive the due reward of our deeds: but this man hath done nothing amiss. And he said unto Jesus, Lord, remember me when thou comest into thy kingdom. And Jesus said unto him, Verily I say unto thee, To day shalt thou be with me in paradise. (Luke 23:38–43 KJV)

Jesus took back the keys of the kingdom and set the saints of old free from hell.

Jesus, when he had cried again with a loud voice, yielded up the ghost. And, behold, the veil of the temple was rent in twain from the top to the bottom; and the earth did quake, and the rocks rent; And the graves were opened; and many bodies of the saints which slept arose, And came out of the graves after his resurrection, and went into the holy city, and appeared unto many. (Matthew 27:50–53 KJV)

But unto every one of us is given grace according to the measure of the gift of Christ. Wherefore he saith, When he ascended up on high, he led captivity captive, and gave gifts unto men. (Now that he ascended, what is it but that he also descended first into the lower parts of the earth? He that descended is the same also that ascended up far above all heavens, that he might fill all things.) (Ephesians 4:7–10 KJV)

Jesus came and fulfilled the law of Moses and then delivered us from the Law of Moses, the Ten Commandments, which are in those Commandments 613 laws, we no longer have to do something to get God to do for us. It is God's grace through Jesus Christ that God will act for us,

> He that spared not his own Son, but delivered
> him up for us all, how shall he not with him also
> freely give us all things? (Romans 8:32 KJV)

> In the end of the sabbath, as it began to dawn
> toward the first day of the week, came Mary
> Magdalene and the other Mary to see the sepul-
> chre. And, behold, there was a great earthquake:
> for the angel of the Lord descended from heaven,
> and came and rolled back the stone from the
> door, and sat upon it. His countenance was like
> lightning, and his raiment white as snow: And
> for fear of him the keepers did shake, and became
> as dead men. And the angel answered and said
> unto the women, Fear not ye: for I know that ye
> seek Jesus, which was crucified. He is not here:
> for he is risen, as he said. Come, see the place
> where the Lord lay. (Matthew 28:1-6 KJV)

Jesus rose up out hell, out of the grave, shedding the grave-clothes off by the power of God. On the third day, He took back the keys of the kingdom from the devil, having all power in heaven and in earth. And He is to give all those who believe in him salvation as a gift, by grace through faith. Jesus redeems us back to God. Without Jesus Christ, no one comes unto God.

> Jesus saith unto him, I am the way, the truth, and
> the life: no man cometh unto the Father, but by
> me. (John 14:6 KJV)

So whenever you are in trouble and have challenges that you cannot bear facing, life crisis even close to death, begin to praise God for who He is and remember that He loves you. The glory of God will show up on your life and through your life, amen.

Here is where you can become God's beloved child:

That if thou shalt confess with thy mouth the Lord Jesus, and shalt believe in thine heart that God hath raised him from the dead, thou shalt be saved. For with the heart man believeth unto righteousness; and with the mouth confession is made unto salvation. (Romans 10:9–10 KJV)

About the Author

Willie J. Brown was granted this story by God to tell about His Son, Jesus Christ, our Lord and Savior. Anyone who reads this book will see that one can be saved through the blood of Jesus Christ, whosoever calls on His name, for God is no longer judging them of their sins—Jesus Christ died on the cross and paid for it all. Therefore, your sins don't take you to hell. However, not accepting Jesus Christ, who died on the cross, in your heart will cause you to lose your soul to hell.

> The Lord is not slack concerning his promise, as some men count slackness; but is longsuffering to us-ward, not willing that any should perish, but that all should come to repentance. (2 Peter 3:9 KJV)

> That if thou shalt confess with thy mouth the Lord Jesus, and shalt believe in thine heart that God hath raised him from the dead, thou shalt be saved. For with the heart man believeth unto righteousness; and with the mouth confession is made unto salvation. (Romans 10:9–10 KJV)

Jesus Christ approved this message.

www.ingramcontent.com/pod-product-compliance
Lightning Source LLC
Chambersburg PA
CBHW020858160726
47993CB00004B/1712